INFINITE
FOOTPRINTS

Daily Wisdom to
Ignite Your Creative Expression in
Walking Your True Path

INFINITE
FOOTPRINTS

Tu Bears and Susan J. Rosenthal

BALBOA.
PRESS
A DIVISION OF HAY HOUSE

Balboa Press books may be ordered through booksellers or by contacting:

Balboa Press
A Division of Hay House
1663 Liberty Drive
Bloomington, IN 47403
www.balboapress.com
1 (877) 407-4847

Because of the dynamic nature of the Internet, any web addresses or
links contained in this book may have changed since publication and
may no longer be valid. The views expressed in this work are solely those
of the author and do not necessarily reflect the views of the publisher,
and the publisher hereby disclaims any responsibility for them.

The author of this book does not dispense medical advice or prescribe the use
of any technique as a form of treatment for physical, emotional, or medical
problems without the advice of a physician, either directly or indirectly. The
intent of the author is only to offer information of a general nature to help
you in your quest for emotional and spiritual well-being. In the event you use
any of the information in this book for yourself, which is your constitutional
right, the author and the publisher assume no responsibility for your actions.

Print information available on the last page.

ISBN: 978-1-5043-7544-3 (sc)
ISBN: 978-1-5043-7545-0 (hc)
ISBN: 978-1-5043-7546-7 (e)

Library of Congress Control Number: 2017935179

Balboa Press rev. date: 04/26/2017

*We dedicate this book to our families, friends and
all the active seekers who wish to experience,
deepen and express their inner truth and infinite joy.*

Table of Contents

Foreword 1

Invitation 7

Timeless Wisdoms and Expressions 11

Day 1   Every Day Is a Celebration 12

Day 2   Take Flight 14

Day 3   A Child's Heart 16

Day 4   Special Gifts 18

Day 5   Destiny's Decision 20

Day 6   An Exceptional Life 22

Day 7   Thanks for the Memories 24

Day 8   Shifting Perception 26

Day 9   Just Be 28

Day 10   Seat of Our Pants 30

Day 11   Sunlight Gratitude 32

Day 12   Time Merges 34

Day 13   Always Enough 36

Day 14   Love Portal 38

Day 15   Own Tune 40

Day 16   Step In 42

Day 17   Measureless Boundaries 44

Day 18   Nothing Stays the Same 46

Day 19   Ebb and Flow 48

Day 20   True Courage 50

Day 21   Letting Go 52

Day 22   Limitless Cooperation 54

Day 23 Evolution Happens 56
Day 24 Celebration Dance...................................58
Day 25 Graceful Perspective...............................60
Day 26 Nature's Peace 62
Day 27 Illuminating Mirror................................64
Day 28 Sitting on a Star 66
Day 29 Threads of Faith 68
Day 30 Pot of Gold 70
Day 31 Tune in a Bucket 72
Day 32 Our Own Magic......................................74
Day 33 Sacred Land 76
Day 34 Stillness Inside 78
Day 35 Seamless Life 80
Day 36 Trusted Footprints 82
Day 37 Reflections..84
Day 38 Breakthrough 86
Day 39 Earthly Connections 88
Day 40 Clean Slate...90
Day 41 Child's Play 92
Day 42 Whispering Wind....................................94
Day 43 Music Festival 96
Day 44 Complexity 98
Day 45 Through an Abyss 100
Day 46 Observance..102
Day 47 Mind Savvy 104
Day 48 Greatness of Heaven..............................106
Day 49 Get Up and Go.......................................108
Day 50 Room For Extraordinary 110
Day 51 Inner Knowing 112
Day 52 Potentials and Possibilities.....................114
Day 53 Crossroads 116
Day 54 Eagles' Grace..118
Day 55 Personal Point of View............................120

Day 56 Awaken Opportunity 122

Day 57 Molding Vision 124

Day 58 Rumbling Voice 126

Day 59 First and Last Moment 128

Day 60 Twenty Years From Now 130

Afterglow 133

About the Authors 137

Acknowledgements 139

Praise for Infinite Footprints 141

More Praise for Infinite Footprints 145

More Available From Infinite Footprints 147

Foreword

When I first heard the title, *Infinite Footprints: Daily Wisdom To Ignite Your Creative Expression in Walking Your True Path*, I received a flash that included the rhythmic sound of boots breaking through the crusty top layer of wintery crisp snow. I saw an image of myself crossing a remote and pristine meadow, a line of footprints behind me and nothing but smooth snow ahead of me. Crunch. Crunch. Crunch. If you've ever spent time in the wilderness in the winter, you know there is a rare, hushed and somewhat disorienting quality that magnifies the sounds of your own breath and footsteps. All is stripped down to you – to the action you are taking, to what you are thinking. You are somehow, at the same time, confronted with a sense of the alarming vastness of possibility, the scary, exciting and strangely unfamiliar vastness.

When confronted with an opportunity to embrace vastness, how many times had I instead crawled into habitual fear, reassuring myself that I could always find my way back to safety by retracing my same old and comfortably familiar steps? What if I allowed a new possibility this time, one which saw the silent expansiveness as a fresh canvas, a place where *Infinite Footprints* could lead anywhere I may want to go? I could make pleasing patterns in the snow, perhaps a labyrinth. I could play and explore. I didn't have to stay on the safe, regular path. I could give myself a wider berth. I could trust myself to find my way home, even without previous footprints to lead the way.

The *Timeless Wisdoms* and *Expressions* offered by Tu Bears and Susan J. Rosenthal in this book are just like that: *you*, singular and magnified, all else whitewashed into the background. *The vastness.* This is about *you*. This is the moment of choosing your next step. What will it be: novel or same, self-doubt or self-love, limited or limitless? Simply in the asking we've opened up a greater opportunity for joy, liberation and expansion to enter in. It is safe to reclaim our powers of manifestation, of will, of imagination, of play, and of *love*. In fact, it is what is being called from us at this critical time on planet Earth: Give yourself a wider berth.

How often do we take the time to reflect on the pattern of footprints we leave behind in our lifetime? For most of us, it has seemed a haphazard path. Our footprints may at first glance seem predetermined by circumstances beyond our control. We may have felt pushed to head in a painful or uncomfortable direction for a time. And yet there has always been a through-line, some sense of direction about what it means to walk in our own integrity and truth. How often do we trust or even take the time to sense that through-line? Sometimes, magically, our steps have felt animated by an intense in-the-moment clarity. We find ourselves gracefully placed again on the through-line. We may experience these moments of grace as deep dives and leaps of faith. We may know them as the sense of peace that comes when we embrace the stillness and listen for what we need. We may experience these moments as a growing ability to sidestep drama, negativity or violence. We may feel these moments as the rush of blood rising like a volcano through us as we stand up and stand our ground with conviction.

Infinite Footprints leads us back again and again to that which is vast and infinite – our spirits, our love, our quantum field of potential from which we came and from which we have never been separated. The reflections gathered in this book are vibrational echoes from our own infinite selves. We know that the value of a rainbow is in beholding its ephemeral beauty, not in engaging the rational mind to postulate its arc, beginning and end, or to explain it as a predictable refraction of light. We have been using the wrong lens to behold ourselves.

When I first read *Timeless Wisdoms*, something amazing happened to me, as I experienced one of those moments of being effortlessly lifted and placed back onto my through-line. It was a shift from head to heart, breakthrough to a place where I perceived myself in the same way I perceive a rainbow, with wonderment and appreciation, experiencing myself directly, not stepping away from myself by objectifying or analyzing who I perceive myself to be. How did it happen? Dr. David Hawkins, M.D., Ph.D., Author of *Letting Go: The Pathway of Surrender,* has shown that words, beyond having meaning, carry a specific vibration that we sense when hearing, reading or thinking them. Dr. Masaru Emoto, Author of *Messages from Water and the Universe,* has shown that simply placing a label with a word such as 'love' or 'hate' on a container of water changes the crystalline structure of the water. What I know is that *Timeless Wisdoms* carries the highest energetic vibrations, feeding us the most nourishing sustenance. Used as a daily reading or made part of any self-care ritual, you will find that the words serve you in ways both seen and unseen, understood and beyond understanding.

At times, the written method of the collections in *Infinite Footprints* resembles that of a jazz musician, crafting combinations that are surprising and discordant enough to defy the brain's insistence on order. The result is that the brain yields, allowing the heart to rush into a void. There is an experience of the expansive and sublime. There have been similar spiritual effects reported by many who adventure into intense, precise in-the-moment concentration such as rock climbers or underwater cave explorers. A mind kept so intensely occupied with a difficult task cannot spill over to control other parts of perception, creating more space for pure, unfiltered direct experience.

As you dive into the inspirational pages that follow, you will notice that you are being invited to have a direct experience of playfulness, surprise, lightness and joy. There is nothing heavy here, but don't let that fool you one bit. If you wish to grasp the enormity of what is being offered, you must challenge yourself to linger a little longer in the doorway of infinite possibility. Dare to be buoyed into fresh territory by bewilderment, whimsy or delight. Your rational mind will not like that. It is accustomed to building walls and categories to contain your thoughts within "safe" and predictable limits. But your essence, your spirit, your soul will absolutely love having more space in which to stretch out, create and play.

My introduction to *Infinite Footprints* came when I met Tu Bears about two years ago as she joined me and a group of women on an online project to develop a companion guidebook to my book, *Enough*. When I read *Infinite Footprints* I recognized the book as a wake up call from home. See what happens when you read the *Timeless Wisdoms* aloud. Can you hear home?

There are many roles to be filled at this time of great transition from the culture of separation to the culture of wholeness and unity. Tu Bears and Susan J. Rosenthal speak as beacons from this infinite territory, encouraging us to embrace all of who we are as essential, enough and beautifully necessary. I invite you into these pages, like a new pair of shoes, to walk beside them on a magical and inspiring journey back to an awareness of your own sacred magnificence. I assure you that no better companion and guide could be found to travel on your personal through-line journey.

Laurie McCammon, MS, Author,
Enough! How to Liberate Yourself and Remake the World with Just One Word

Invitation

All of us walk this earth for 86,400 seconds each day. Who we are in every moment, all our thoughts and beliefs held, emotions felt, and actions taken are infinite footprints, both deliberately and unknowingly left behind.

These footprints tell our stories of who we are, what we do while here, and what we leave as a legacy. They are our individual marks on the vast canvas of life. Relatives and ancestors pass through our DNA, adding their essence to our footprints. We create our individual path, a journey of expressing ourselves in the ever-expanding present moment.

Our footprints are uniquely ours. No one else on the planet can step in our tracks. We unveil and experience things about ourselves that only we will ever know. There is great promise in what we understand of our journey, and on a deeper level, a daily self-mastery that reminds us how powerful we really are.

Throughout each day, we have opportunities to explore our sense of self, connect with our true inner being, and open up to possibilities for broader awakening and presence. *Infinite Footprints: Daily Wisdom To Ignite Your Creative Expression in Walking Your True Path* provides a framework to grow self-knowledge, self-acceptance, self-love and self-trust as we awaken to our fullest potential.

Provocative, stimulating and transformative, the poetic

prose of the *Timeless Wisdoms* awakens and invites us into our multi-dimensional inner world of thoughts, emotions, beliefs and choices. Each daily wisdom provides contemplation for the day. It awakens soulful parts to consider new perspectives of an inner intelligence that bypasses our mind and touches our heart core. What we value in our lives becomes our guiding principles. Exploring personal values is a key that unlocks gates to living an authentic life, aligning with our destiny, and laying down our infinite footprints.

When I met Tu Bears several years ago, I was profoundly moved by the expansive spirit and wisdom she embodies, far beyond her human presence. I envisioned combining our knowledge and experiences in supporting and uplifting others by building a community for people seeking to discover, creatively express, and live their inner truth.

To personalize *Infinite Footprints* and make them interactive for readers, we collaborated on creating a three-step process. Reading the *Timeless Wisdom* is the first step. *Expression* is the second step. Through exploratory questions and statements, *Expression* provides an opportunity to apply the wisdom to our daily lives, release any burdens, blocks and pains, and express whatever our heart or mind wishes in our outer world. The blank space that follows *Expression* allows us to intimately explore our deep knowing and feeling, a place to capture impressions, thoughts, feelings and dreams through writing, sketching, doodling, collage and other forms of self-expression.

Journaling for a few minutes each day gives direction and has a powerful impact on expanding our commitment to personal awareness and transformation. To write a few lines or create an image that defines an experience or thought, describes an idea, pulls forth an inner knowing, or even invokes the taste of something delicious, brings insight and ownership to our life journey.

At the bottom of each blank space, we've included a thoughtful gratitude to complete the *Infinite Footprints* process. Through declaring our grateful intention to be our best selves and celebrate the paths that we forge, we affirm our commitment to ourselves, our purpose, and our places on Earth.

As a tool to grow, reflect and express ourselves that takes just moments each day, *Infinite Footprints* opens us up, revitalizes us, and helps us navigate life. It shows us the fullness of ourselves to consciously awaken, build strength, generate passion, and raise awareness of all that we are. As co-creators of our lives, we see that one day's thoughts and actions turn into the next day's results and consequences.

Be bold. Walk on in joy and serenity. Leave your own indelible footprints on our planet.

Susan J. Rosenthal, MBA
Business Leader, Speaker, Coach, Intuitive Healer

Timeless Wisdoms
and Expressions

Each one of you is alive with a great purpose. There is no mistake. You may not live as if you are someone else or walk as if you belong somewhere else. You cannot expect another to be who you are. You were born to know these things about yourself. You must know your purpose, you must live your truth, and you are required to walk gently upon Mother Earth. Each one of you is here on this land, in this world and inside this universe, to live as your soul guides you forward in destiny's infinite footprints.

–Elder Woman
A Shakchi Humma

Day 1

Every Day Is a Celebration

Timeless Wisdom: There are a multitude of reasons to celebrate. Each day is as monumental as any other. We have tremendous opportunities to speak out, give rise to harmony in moments of conflict, set the record straight, and spearhead campaigns of conscious forgiveness, mindful rejuvenation, and awakened celebration. Every day can be filled to overflowing with gratitude. May we take notice, and whisper a simple *thank you* with each step. Every minute equals 60 chances an hour. In a 24-hour period we have 1,440 opportunities to demonstrate our gratitude.

Expression: What are ways that you celebrate your life? Create a plan for a celebration filled to overflowing with gratitude for your favorite people and ways to have fun.

Today is filled with gratitude for your favorite people and enjoyments.

Day 2

Take Flight

Timeless Wisdom: There are infinite creative possibilities in every moment. Our days are filled with explorative intersections. Upon waking from a deep slumber, we are human beings slipping from our cocoons and exploring the opportunities of the new day. Like butterflies, we might take flight in any direction. Let's just say, sleep is a purification ceremony and an act of forgiveness and reconnection. Wakefulness is a spiritual emergence, a birth of new life. It is ours to investigate and research every new possibility. We each awaken to our greatness of personal character, attitude and disposition. Use every ounce of courage you have to spread your wings and fly!

Expression: Close your eyes and realize that you have wings to fly in new directions. Write down the things you want to fly toward, and give yourself time to think about them.

Acknowledge your thankfulness in how you learned to fly.

Day 3

A Child's Heart

Timeless Wisdom: There are no fences or limits on magical enlightenment in an original mind. May we gift every child the freedom to express the infinite wisdom he or she came to this planet with. Let the child within each of us slow down enough to truly examine each repeated belief we claim as ours. It may be time to clear our thoughts of old patterns and listen to our deepest wisdom from a childlike heart. Releasing habitual beliefs of fear and restriction handed to us awakens the freedom to celebrate and desire to express our own convictions.

Expression: Is every belief or opinion you were taught an authentic feeling or truth for you? Do the miraculous today. Release yourself from a habit and write about it.

Your inner child will show you what it is most thankful for.

Day 4

Special Gifts

Timeless Wisdom: Clear thinking requires training. First we learn what other people think. They teach us and we grow up believing they're right. Then we discover on our own that we are not in harmony with their teachings. Our personal journey is finding our truest purpose, being authentic, and allowing our individuality to express its realness. May we live our own truth and accept the diverse paths of others. Let us realize that each person has a personal gift that we are all destined to express and share. It is our daily choice to live in harmony, balance and grace in our diversified universe.

Expression: Create a list of what you discovered as your gifts of authentic expression. Write how you might share them with others.

Feel gratitude for all you have discovered.

Day 5

Destiny's Decision

Timeless Wisdom: Destiny, free will, and the decisions we choose move us through life, create a magnetic field around us, and perceive the road in front of us. Often we do things or we manage choices that distract us from our true destiny. Many times we are crashing, colliding, leaving things behind, or backtracking to figure out why things didn't go the way we wanted. Within each of us is an internal pace, personal rhythm, and honest groove. May we seek to coordinate our actions with our intimate natural being in full color. Mother Earth's truest character is to gracefully contain all living things. Our human contributions are in alignment with our own destiny and Mother Earth's truth as we balance in her gifts and joyfully trip the light fantastic.

Expression: Take a few minutes to gather your thoughts about destiny. Write what a balanced scenario between yourself and Mother Nature feels like to you.

*Allow your destiny to contribute to
Mother Nature with appreciation.*

Day 6

An Exceptional Life

Timeless Wisdom: Each new day is an opportunity to envision or recreate our circumstances into a flourishing, more vibrant life. There is room for being extraordinary within whom we have become and where we conceive ourselves to live, work and play. We continue expanding our visionary skills to embrace positive self-worth, excellent health, nourishing relationships, fulfilling work, and wholesome environments. Each of us is fashioned of star qualities, and we possess the power to design an exceptional life just because we are.

Expression: Make a list of your personal talents and gifts. Read them aloud and send the energy of each into your atmosphere, claiming its power.

Let yourself be thankful for your natural star qualities.

Day 7

Thanks for the Memories

Timeless Wisdom: Giving rise to freedom and moving forward often requires looking back. In a brisk wind we tend to put our head down, tuck it under, and drag the burdens with us. What if we take a minute to turn around, say "thank you" to the memories we are hanging onto, lay them down at the side of the road we are traveling to lighten our load, and face the future with much less baggage? Every memory is a jumping off place to a new future. With a breath and a smile, thank your memories for the lessons they brought and the dreams they inspired.

Expression: Think about a challenging time in your life, say "thank you", and choose to let it go. Write a letter to yourself describing how you are leaving your past behind and taking steps in the direction of your envisioned future.

Celebrate your memories and their gifts with gratitude.

Day 8

Shifting Perception

Timeless Wisdom: From our point of observation on a clear day, each of us will view the world from an individual perspective. Even having seen what is right in front of us, we are undecided about what may actually be there. From one millisecond to the next, there is change. Within our thoughts, there is resistance to a possibility of looking through a different lens and witnessing molecular movement. In the most infinitesimal radiant looking glass, we may only see what our limited mind experience can accept as real in this moment. May we remind ourselves that continual shifts in perception occur to stretch beyond our mind's current observation, and to consider what may be yet unknown.

Expression: Notice an idea that frequently crosses your mind. Write an affirmation expanding your belief of this idea and a purpose for it to grow into potentiality.

Let your mind's expansiveness bring you gratitude.

Day 9

Just Be

Timeless Wisdom: When we hold too tightly to our position, we are often left with nothing. Life around us is moving swiftly; one day we are in the know, and the next, *the known* has jumped to somewhere unknown. Our inner truth is simple, stable, self-assured, and eternal. We often believe the ego personality is our truest identity. We may invest great effort into proving this to be factual. We claim an identity and create an image until the rug gets pulled out from under us. The soul never has to prove a thing. May we courageously come out of hiding, fearlessly be our truest selves, and confidently give others the opportunity and comfort to *be* their honest selves when around us. Realize the gift of *being*.

Expression: Connect with your sense of *being*. Write, draw or create a collage that demonstrates your truest sense of *being*.

Give thanks for your own understanding
of who you truly are.

Day 10

Seat of Our Pants

Timeless Wisdom: Sometimes we can't tell if we are coming or going and life is too short to get upset about much of anything. Mostly we are flying by the seat of our pants down a road that takes us out to the universe. On a moon's roundabout, we travel through cycles until an ocean's tide tugs our knickers into a twist. We can't forget to smile when we hear the bells jingle on the ice cream truck and watch for the mud puddles at the end of the day. We surely remembered to bring our work gloves, our waders, and a shovel. No telling whom else we might meet along the way.

Expression: Explore how you may be moving through life by the seat of your pants. Write about what this experience has taught you.

Feel your gratitude for flying by the seat of your pants.

Day 11

Sunlight Gratitude

Timeless Wisdom: We stand with open arms in the warm rays of the sun. As a daily ritual, we gather energy through our feet from Mother Earth, and from the sun's illumination, as much as we can contain. We feel grateful as our vital life force fills to the point of overflowing. We know we must be discerning in how we use this universal power. Our intentions along the path determine our giving, as well as our receiving. Let us radiate and illuminate as we give generously and invite others to receive our gifts.

Expression: Silently stand in the sunlight for a few minutes. Feel the energy from earth and sky, and let your body collect the vibrational power. Write about these feelings.

Invoke your thankfulness for the natural elements of our universe.

Day 12

Time Merges

Timeless Wisdom: The beginning of time intimately knows the end of time. They meet as they complete the circle and merge into one state: timelessness. Only when one season disappears do we realize there is and has always been enough time. A continuation of movement in a circle of no beginning and no end is our truest rhythmic discovery. All motion is in the present. May we merge our points of separation into the wholeness of one harmoniously balanced being.

Expression: Envision yourself holding one end of a rope in your left hand, and your family members encircling you holding a part of the same rope. Clasping the rope's other end in your right hand, visualize yourself as both the beginning and the end of the circle. Draw this image and your feelings about it.

Feel gratitude knowing you are the
beginning and end of your life's circle.

Day 13

Always Enough

Timeless Wisdom: There is a ray of hope, an enlightened moment between each obstacle placed so strategically along our path. Our soul's journey into an unknown world becomes known the minute our heart begins to welcome our innate greatness and wholeness. Greatness is naturally ours from birth. We are enough, we have enough, every step is enough, and every smile is enough. Our soul's journey is exactly right. Even in adversity we can handle it. We are fully equipped for every step on destiny's path.

Expression: Meditate on your soul's journey and realize you are always enough. Write, draw or simply doodle all the ways that you are enough.

Choose an experience today to appreciate being enough.

Day 14

Love Portal

Timeless Wisdom: We all came from people who experienced unconditional love in a cosmic doorway. Each of us has the ability to walk through these passageways to receive the love that is available; yet, often we are too afraid to step through the opening. We choose to remain stuck in what we know and what we have, and find ourselves in the quicksand of discomfort. Suffering and struggle are all too familiar, and they create pain and heartache. It takes one decision, one step, and one choice to let go of the past and move forward toward our destiny. Let us choose to love ourselves unconditionally, and forgive all past emotional attachments and addictions. We can invoke the cosmic portal to entice us to step fully into our lightness of being.

Expression: Think about how you feel when you connect with your family lineage, both known and unknown. Let your mind drift among them and feel their support. Create a drawing, collage or your family tree.

Whisper thankful words for the love that created you.

Day 15

Own Tune

Timeless Wisdom: In our own rhythm, we glide or stroll from one event to another. We often go along with a crowd, find ourselves in an unnatural flow, and wake up in someone else's concept of life. A scale of notes on a page may prompt us to write our own music, to dance to our favorite tunes, and to sing our original song. In the moments of our days let us remind ourselves to hum a few bars of our own melody and sing the chorus of our truest self.

Expression: Think about the music that runs through your head and ask yourself what is special about that particular piece of music. Write about how it relates to you and if it reflects your true being.

Express gratitude for the music you sincerely enjoy.

Day 16

Step In

Timeless Wisdom: Along our path from birth to death there will be a secret door for each of us. It waits to be discovered. The portal often appears when we least expect it and feels like a miracle. A hidden entrance to our truest journey could materialize on a crowded street, behind a worn-out barn, adjacent to a mountain trail, or right in our own backyard. We must read between the lines, be ready and courageous, and have the will to be fully conscious without turning back. There are no do overs. When the sun sets it is done. Be ready when the doorway opens and step in with both feet.

Expression: Look back over your life and see if there were moments of openings or passageways to your inner journey. Did you wonder about them, walk away from them, or walk through them? Act them out physically, and then write about them.

*Feel grateful for the moments when you
can read between the lines.*

Day 17

Measureless Boundaries

Timeless Wisdom: There are paper-thin lines between the worlds as we travel on the wind. A human soul moves through circumstance of half-broken and oftentimes unexpected splits in ethereal realities. Decades of ancestors drift amid the heard and unheard, whispering stories we may have forgotten. Our totems, spirit guides, deities and angels reach through a veil to prompt us at the crossroads, drop a book from a shelf in front of us, or motivate a person to say a meaningful word. We are not alone. We must set clear intentions while measureless space travels light years through the Milky Way into the Earth's atmosphere to manifest our aspirations. Listen closely to wisdom passing by, speak clearly, and walk fearlessly with grace while traversing the cosmos without boundaries.

Expression: Write about a time when you felt half-broken. Call upon your spirit helpers and ask for courage to accept that you are complete and whole in every way. Write about your new chosen thoughts and feelings.

Be grateful for change and your courage to go with the flow.

Day 18

Nothing Stays the Same

Timeless Wisdom: On a road less traveled, where it appears there may not be much happening, it turned out to be a glorious night of tightrope walking over a rainbow. We are sure to take an umbrella because, of course, anything could change in an instant. The laws of nature dictate that nothing stays the same. What was true yesterday was nowhere to be found today. For sure, what came around today won't even take the time to show up tomorrow. Dance with the unexpected and celebrate the opportunity for change.

Expression: Write about the changes that have occurred in your life. Accept and embrace all that has brought you to this moment in life, to this latest version of you. Skip, jump, laugh and yell, "Hallelujah"!

Hallelujah is a multitude of thankful jubilations. Bring it on!

Day 19

Ebb and Flow

Timeless Wisdom: The more determined we are to hold onto our attachments and our limited thinking, the more challenging the world feels. The universe is constantly changing with or without our opinions or approvals. The harder we dig in, the more stuck we become. May we go with the ebb and flow, and be in the present moment when and where the opportunities show up. Let us dance gracefully through life's flowing current.

Expression: Examine your attachment to a person, object, job or location with loving-kindness toward yourself, and what you feel attached to. Write about why you feel it is special to you. Dance gracefully around the emotions. Choose to keep its specialness or use the energy to create who you are becoming.

Dance gracefully in a circle of gratitude.

Day 20

True Courage

Timeless Wisdom: A collection of small fears creates a net. The more we fear, the tighter the weave. The mesh allows air and water to easily slip through, and still the fear holds tight. We can untangle our nets of fright, apprehension and foreboding with wise tools. There is true magic in our courage, bravery and strength. We are ready to receive a deeper faith to interlace our confidence, wholehearted joy, and personal faith with our bold awareness.

Expression: Write three fears you have used to build traps for yourself. Write three of your strengths that could move you toward being courageous. Ask your inner self to assist in releasing the fears that no longer serve your best self. Choose to focus on your strengths going forward.

Shout a big "Thank You" for the courage you have gathered.

Day 21

Letting Go

Timeless Wisdom: The sky coasted, puffed, folded, was sprinkled with clouds and sang lyrics we couldn't remember. The sun tiptoed lightly, sneaking away to a cabaret for the rest of the night. It is all about transformation, hands, bones, skin, hearts and change. Let go, forget yesterday, wait for tomorrow, give it up, and leave control freak concepts to their own demise. Walk away, fly over, pass it by, forget the lyrics, doo-wop doo-wop fa-la-la and write a new song to sing.

Expression: Take a walk or sit on the porch and breathe in the day. Write down a few lyrics that unite you with nature surrounding you.

Sing your true song of grateful inspiration.

Day 22

Limitless Cooperation

Timeless Wisdom: Cosmic nature cooperates with each tiny particle in the earth's molecular structure. The human mind is in complete alignment with every rambling thought traveling across electrical neurons in our mortal fabric. Our habitual patterns fall under the original constructed jurisdiction. Choice belongs to each individual within the framework of historical theories. Ideas, beliefs and perceptions present new concepts to outdated thoughts, and the battles begin. We can be fully aware of what we are truly choosing in every single minute.

Expression: It is never too late to change your mind and co-create a new dream. Allow your mind to merge with cosmic expansion, and draw or write what your new vision represents to you.

Reach for the sky and whisper "thank you"
for being who you are.

Day 23

Evolution Happens

Timeless Wisdom: Transformational evolution happens in the simplest of moments. When we least expect anything can possibly change, it does. Mother Earth is our great gift as the giver of things magical, practical and medicinal. We interact with and affect our surroundings and often disrupt her natural gifts. It is rare that we offer gratitude for what we take from her, learn from her, or receive from her. Mother Earth is alive. She is the most ancient of wisdoms, memory, and the most resourceful at restoring herself to balance. Everyday is a good day to honor our planet, to sing to her, to drum in time with her heartbeat, and to teach our children of her history and wisdom.

Expression: Gather objects that represent the gifts of Mother Earth and appreciate how they have evolved over time. Sing, laugh, shout or dance about your own beautiful gifts. Then, write about them.

Everything comes from Mother Earth.
Feel grateful for all she has given.

Day 24

Celebration Dance

Timeless Wisdom: A little bit of this and a tiny bit more of that. Jump on a 4-wheeler, watch out for the prairie dogs, and wake up the coyotes. Happiness on any given day sticks around longer, makes us hoop, holler and sing. Our singing chases away the rattlesnakes and gives us more to be thankful for. Magic happens when the stars come out to play and we put some cedar on our campfire. May the women pick up their skirts, kick up their heels, and show the children how to dance. Let our brothers, uncles, fathers and sons dance a two-step and yell enthusiastically. Before we know it, morning will come and our grandmas will put on the coffee pot and make a big breakfast.

Expression: Call forth your spirit of celebration. What causes you to kick up your heels? Get out your colored pens, pencils or crayons and create a banner of a laughing family, dancing crowd, or whatever makes you smile with glee.

*In your celebration, give thanks for all
times past, present and future.*

Day 25

Graceful Perspective

Timeless Wisdom: Looking at life a little too closely could cause us to get caught up in the small stuff. Perspective and the point of view from our backyard might prevent us from seeing what is happening in the front yard. Running with the crowd, sitting in the chair where we always sit in a meeting, or choosing the same coffee drink limits our potential prospects. There could be something said for switching things around, shifting the way we look at the same old crowd, changing up the conversation, and scanning the menu for something wild and free. Broadening our scope of things may spark our creative muscle and expand our visionary horizons.

Expression: How has grace shown up in your life? Feel its presence now, write about how it feels, and then send it outward to others.

Hold appreciation for any moment of grace in your day.

Day 26

Nature's Peace

Timeless Wisdom: We follow the way of nature as if it were our map, our guide through each day. Nature encompasses every tiny detail of our being, from the smallest cell throughout the cosmos. Each of us contains the universe within. There is a flow, a path, a river, a simple tree, a tiny houseplant, or a fish in a bowl to remind us of our personal spiritual journey. Days, months and years go by and we continue co-mingling with a natural way of being. The threads of time braid and weave our lives, our families, our co-workers, our likes and dislikes, and our past, present and future into nature. May we honestly live, patiently accept, freely love, and peacefully live in harmony with all nature.

Expression: Write about or draw your favorite aspects of nature, why they are meaningful to you, and how nature touches your heart.

Feel deep gratitude for your natural surroundings.

Day 27

Illuminating Mirror

Timeless Wisdom: In our cosmic makeup of luminescent networks every molecular particle is divinely created. Each vibrant piece contains an intricate hologram of the entire universal structure. There are no mistakes within our energetic field of existence. Our ultimate, unlimited personal sphere is an exact replica of all creation. We are united with all living things. An expanded universe rolls through time and space in an offering of pure, uncomplicated fancy. Precisely the moment we accept our destiny universal forces align in complete harmony to support our awakened surroundings. We generate an ability to invoke compassionate change, tip the balancing scale, and enliven our truest gifts. It is all an illumination of harmonic wholeness.

Expression: Consider yourself a part of the whole universe and in harmony with all things. Write about how it feels to fit in and to be exactly where you are meant to be.

Display your appreciation for your wholeness.

Day 28

Sitting on a Star

Timeless Wisdom: Living, breathing and being is the Great Mystery of Heaven and Earth. On any given day we are surrounded by mundane chores entangled among the ordinary, while comingling with the phenomenal. There exists the extraordinary within the daily doing. We find illumination in fine company with common routine. It is up to us to generate enlightenment in whatever the day offers us along our personal path. It could be time to stand up and examine the stars quietly covered in secret threads of our inner strengths and core values. We can take a moment to breathe in every bright particle of our authentic radiance.

Expression: Give yourself time to think about your gifts, unnoticed talents, and simple things you naturally do without thinking about it. Write these down knowing you are made of the same cosmic wonder in every star in the sky, and just as bright.

Appreciate your gifts and give thanks
when others notice your talents.

Day 29

Threads of Faith

Timeless Wisdom: Among threads of our existence are fragments of our history, successes, insecurities, secrets, grief and every other aspect of our lives. Each piece of who we are weaves the legend of who we were and who we will become. We can recognize the habitual links that keep us repeating patterns that no longer serve our enlightened destiny, and choose a more vibrantly alive alternative. Our personal fears create the impossibilities ahead of us. Our internal faith gives rise to new possibilities. Let us be extremely grateful to recognize our patterns thread by thread, choose inner wisdom, and strengthen threads of kindness, hope and faith.

Expression: Gather your colored pencils or pens. Draw lines, both horizontal and vertical, representing your personal weaving. On some lines, use words that come to mind to represent important pieces of your history. On other lines, represent your present day. Use the drawing as a reflection of how far you have come, and a design of where you would like to be.

From a place of expanded vision, amplify
your appreciation to dream big.

Day 30

Pot of Gold

Timeless Wisdom: It is a glorious night for tightrope walking on a moonbeam. We gather our specialties, grab our umbrellas, and toss our fates to the wind. Technology attached at the hip, we can be there before you can shake a stick. As long as your cat doesn't step on the mute button, we could hear everything you've got on your mind. The Internet cloud is circling the globe with private passwords and electrical holding tanks. A buzzing current pollutes airways. It could be time to put on the flying goggles, strap on our cardboard wings, lift some spirits, and conjure angels.

Expression: Gather your loose change, put it in a bag, take it to the nearest bank and cash it in. Draw a rainbow and write the total amount 100 times on a pot at the end of your rainbow, and visualize the amount growing 1,000 times bigger. Have a belly laugh and let the universe do the rest.

Appreciate what is appearing in your personal pot of gold.

Day 31

Tune in a Bucket

Timeless Wisdom: It is a marvel, a wonder of astonishment, when a paddleboat makes a turn at a fork in a muddy creek as sunlight is changing colors. It is almost like someone wrote a song, lyrics of celebration, and strummed across an old guitar in time with blood pumping through our hearts. All it would take to make the day perfect would be a sweet harmonica cabaletta as a blue heron lifted out of the water. Wide-eyed, slick, croaking bullfrogs can't hold a tune in a bucket perched on a lily pad. Never you mind, we'll put on our waders, stomp down the river bottoms, and go fishing in a crawdad hole.

Expression: Recall two or four lines of your favorite song and write them down. Hum them out of tune. Then lift your head up and sing them just the way you would like them to sound.

With the melody of your favorite song,
create a verse of appreciation.

Day 32

Our Own Magic

Timeless Wisdom: We travel on a simple road through valleys, across rivers, and over crusty layers where we discover the magic of who we truly are. There is an unexplored place deeply rooted in cosmic authenticity, an ingenious gathering of universal wisdom in the very center of our original self. It is a neat little package all tied up with ribbons that many of us are afraid to open. Some of us were courageous enough to peek and closed it right back up for fear others might not like us if they knew what was hidden there. We could run on for a long time without being true to ourselves. The vibration of universal cosmic wisdom is now connecting to a bigger picture. It is our individual responsibility to open our soulful, authentic self and *be* originally natural. We can be brave enough to live our truest purpose, the sooner the better. It is never too late to open up to our own magic.

Expression: Take some time to sit alone with your thoughts and peek inside your truest self. Explore and write down what you see.

*Write a thoughtful thank you note for
your wondrous innate wisdom.*

Day 33

Sacred Land

Timeless Wisdom: We are awestruck and humbled when our feet walk on holy land. Kindred spirits hold hands out for one another in moments where there are no words left to speak. In a vision of heaven's lightning, our hearts skip a beat. We notice a difference in how we feel, and gratitude dances freely through our veins. Fire and blood transcend on subatomic levels of changing times. We are called to attention between ancient sacred honoring and quantum leaping into an explosive spiritual evolution on planet Earth. Our hearts cry for peaceful common ground. We are here to create sacred space wherever we are at any given moment.

Expression: Are there places you have been that felt special to you? Describe the feelings that come to mind and honor their gifts.

Create a gift or an offering to honor a
place on earth that is holy to you.

Day 34

Stillness Inside

Timeless Wisdom: In our world of elaborate plans and overdone agendas, we discover opportunities of natural silence in passing breezes. Let us bring our awareness in the moment to a centered place of stillness, a realized recognition of our inner quiet, and place our attention there. In the midst of a family dilemma, chaotic meeting, irritating crowded room, or interrupting quarrel, we can take a deep breath and go inward to our heartbeat. We are filled with illuminating peace from the inside out.

Expression: Stillness comes naturally, yet we forget how organic it feels to be internally quiet. Fill a clear glass half full with water and place it in front of you. Imagine yourself as that still, undisturbed water in the glass. Write how it feels to be quiet inside.

Be thankful for the stillness in your day.

Day 35

Seamless Life

Timeless Wisdom: Beneath the surface, the clock is ticking and covered in mud. We are slipping through superficial noise, catching on strings of words that mean nothing, attaching our every hope to a puff of smoke. We twist, turn and run as fast as we can, jumping fences until our feet get caught in barbed wire. The ancestors remind us to read the vibrations across water and listen to whispers on the wind. It could be so. With a little help, we could slide over time's mystery, forget to be human, and live seamlessly through earth and sky. A mystical life force drives us forward or slings us backward. A clock covered in mud keeps a heartbeat whether anyone else believes in us or not. We must wholeheartedly believe in our vision as a seamless destiny.

Expression: Explore your seamless life inside, and notice places where you have felt disjointed breaks and pieces. Reconnect the pieces, stand in your wholeness, regain your confidence, and see your own perfection. Draw a circle and then notice you are whole with no beginning or end in your life.

Celebrate your own completeness.

Day 36

Trusted Footprints

Timeless Wisdom: We are walking a path of self-remembrance. Yes, there are others walking with us, before us, behind us, and a few beside us. Yet, every step is individually ours - unique, careful or clumsy. The footprints we leave belong only to us. Sure we can follow another's concepts, even share our own ideas. But the long and short of it is, we are completely responsible for our individual choices, actions and judgments. It is worthwhile to sincerely pay attention to what is deep inside our own soul, trust our feet to know the way, hold our heads high, and keep on stepping. Remember, others have their own steps to manage without our interference. *Help* only works if we do it without thinking we know what's best. And *help* could mean we all fall down.

Expression: Think about where you have been and where you are going. Do you feel equipped to stay the path, trust your direction, and allow others to follow their own path? Write about your ability to trust yourself fully.

Demonstrate gratitude for your instinctual choices along your pathway.

Day 37

Reflections

Timeless Wisdom: We are surrounded with mirrors. With every thought there appears a reflection. In our families' eyes, we saw our image, a clone of ourselves when we heard the voices of our children repeat what we have said to them. An entire universe embodied and duplicated our opinions, ideas and beliefs. Mass collective, cosmic debris in the minds of many, rendered all of us in a Jeopardy Daily Double, like twin replicas of credence, we declared either for or against. We began with coherent insight, wise perception, discerning awareness, and enlightened clarity about what we choose to think, speak, see and know.

Expression: Place a mirror in front of you and a lit candle between you and the mirror. Look into the mirror through the candlelight. Slowly change your expression from a smile to a frown and any other face you want to see. Notice how the candle reflects your images, and write about your feelings.

Embody your grateful heart and see light in your eyes.

Day 38

Breakthrough

Timeless Wisdom: Awareness is the source of all that is, was and will ever be. We give ourselves permission to become more aware of our surroundings and stretch our potential into our greatest ecstasy. When we break through to our soul's depth or our mind's vision, our internal perception increases our acceptance and creates wisdom. It is our time to break through patterns and habits, and open our minds to listen closer, see beyond, touch more, taste out of the ordinary, and breathe deeper. Unlimited possibilities begin with expanded thinking. There is always more to learn.

Expression: Habits and patterns are like barbed wire fences. Give yourself space for a breakthrough. Write about a habit or limit you put upon yourself, and see if possible ideas come to you about a way to break through.

Appreciate breaking your patterns and what has been holding you back.

Day 39

Earthly Connections

Timeless Wisdom: We stand before a new day with a beginner's mind, listening, watching and learning. There is a deep knowing that comes with every signal from our surroundings. All of life is connected. On the wind we hear our directions, guidance and assurance. Standing on the earth grants us an opportunity to merge with Mother Earth's heartbeat and stabilize our feelings. Watching a campfire, we unite with our passion and the flames of our inner truth. We meet our new day as a student of life, seeking to embrace our earthly connections while reaching out for one another. It is our time to hold hands around the world in peaceful solidarity.

Expression: How do you best experience your personal connections to Mother Earth? Write about the things in nature that bring you strength, peace and comfort.

Express appreciation for the nature that surrounds you.

Day 40

Clean Slate

Timeless Wisdom: Rise up from the waters of mediocrity to shout the miracles among the living. Rise up with more enthusiastic esprit de corps than life has ever known. Shed the skin that held us back; release the sadness, guilt and shame that were placed onto us like a mourning veil by those who worshipped a god of sins. Forgive our ignorance and hateful blame, forgive, forgive and forgive again. Rise up a newborn, welcome a clean slate, and stretch toward the sky like a sunflower in summer. Yell as the eagle soars and rejoice our days ahead. Rise up, we say, be comfortable in all things original and unprecedented. Our life can be full of miracles.

Expression: An act of forgiveness is like erasing words on a black board. With a clean slate we have an opportunity to write a new script. Make a list of important features you would like in your new script.

Bubble over with gratitude for your clean slate and the steps ahead of you.

Day 41

Child's Play

Timeless Wisdom: A burst of creative color, a fresh flamboyant wind, and a garden full of blooming flowers opened our minds to choices, options and flexibility. In our surroundings we have been oversaturated with linear, rule-based thinking that often made it difficult to see our truest choices, other options, and possible flexibilities. We are ready for a healthy, peaceful, creative, open-minded environment. Future generations depend on us to create an educational system that can expand children's options, establish security, and encourage each child to live authentically from beginning to end. We can follow the path of nature by operating a changeable, adaptable, expansive, brilliantly diverse system. We can plant colorful seeds of greatness by rearranging our surroundings and flexing our imagination.

Expression: Use colored pencils or photos cut from magazines to visualize an ideal creative environment for children at play. Let your inner child frolic around the page.

Laugh with thankfulness and childlike
innocence for your imagination.

Day 42

Whispering Wind

Timeless Wisdom: Hidden in cloudy shadows are opportunities of unknown origin and golden mysteries for deep reflection. There are great fishing spots waiting for shoelaces with frayed ends, and rubber ducks bobbling above the water watching out for otters floating by on their backs. It is a night of whispering wind stories we've only wished for around a campfire. We get out auntie's fruit jars with holes poked in the lid to catch our fireflies. Don't forget a quick wash off in the claw foot tub before we wink at the moon and dream, wrapped in velvet blankets wearing silk pajamas.

Expression: Listen to your inner child full of bright imagination, and write your own fairytale with colored pencils.

With a twinkle in your eye, give appreciation to your inner child.

Day 43

Music Festival

Timeless Wisdom: Life comes in many forms. Oftentimes we miss which matrix passed by. There in front of us floating like an angel, crossing wires with Jimi Hendrix and Elvis, we are watching out for Janis Joplin on a skateboard. Sparks begin to fly from John Lennon's hula hoop, while Ringo Starr runs through the sprinklers with his microphone shorting out. Yep, just like heaven, anything can happen on a string of tales across clouds and blue sky. We never give up on music and we are ready to dance.

Expression: Create a list of your favorite musicians, singers and songs. Write about how music makes you feel. Carve out time today to listen to your all-time treasured recordings.

*Sing a grateful song from your heart for
the wonder of music in your life.*

Day 44

Complexity

Timeless Wisdom: There was a complex, bohemian, wise woman traveling over the airwaves. We knew it took time to cut to the chase, and we put together some homemade mud pies. We told the witch doctor to flip the circuit breaker, rotate the spinning wheel, and fire up the satellite dish. We certainly got it under control while we watched one more day bite the dust. There are no absolutes; we didn't get it all done today. We'll get up early and give it our best shot tomorrow.

Expression: As your mind flips a switch from one crazy thought to the next, give yourself a break. Downshift gears to travel at a slower pace to be able to breathe. Tell your mind to follow your breath... inhale, pause, exhale, pause and do it again for two minutes. Pick one image that rattles in your mind and write about it playfully.

Explore how grateful you can be for the
craziness rambling in your mind.

Day 45

Through an Abyss

Timeless Wisdom: We are reaching into the darkness in a field of all possibilities. We are looking for the next great opportunity. There is a clear intention, an undying conviction to motivate us to dive over the edge feet first. Destiny pulls us closer to our dreams. There is no turning back, and no other way except to go through it. People say, "What doesn't kill us only makes us stronger." Every event, experience and circumstance transports us to the next right move. Time and time again we ask for nothing less than inspiration, and hold onto our skirts and shirttails before we jump into the abyss. Some of us drag our feet; a few of us jump right in and cast caution to the wind. It is great to realize we have arrived. We are certainly worthy to be here.

Expression: Marvel at the realization that you are here and you are worthy. Notice how far you have come. Write a letter of congratulations to yourself, mentioning the darkness you endured, and how you were transported by your circumstances.

Be thankful to your creative genius for having gone through an abyss.

Day 46

Observance

Timeless Wisdom: Destiny surrounds us with opportunity. How we choose to relate to it creates the journey we are on. Authenticity requires diligence, consistency, and a certain amount of finesse. We are quickly maneuvering our way around the rocks of hardship, differences, darkness, and oftentimes, hatefulness. Within the core of our authentic being lives a witness, a watcher with no attachment to the emotional this and that. It is greatly possible this could be the wise one we seek. From that space of observance, our world is steady, quiet and flowing. In our center of stillness there is no anxiety, upset, torment, or mean demons chasing us. May we follow our gentle breath, inhale and exhale in constant solitude to that sacred place within. Let us begin to see that no matter what the situation, our destiny is at hand.

Expression: Here is a day of observance, stand back and witness, allow anxiety, arguments and fear to pass you by. Let yourself watch mindfully without any emotional attachment. Write about what you felt while in witness mode, and leave judgment out of it.

*Smile with gratefulness for what you
witnessed in your experience.*

Day 47

Mind Savvy

Timeless Wisdom: May we question structure, probe framework, and turn over every rock to uncover our own unique reason for having dysfunctional, upsetting, dramatic outbursts. Give us the wherewithal, new wisdom to rattle our cages, and dig through the DNA until we resolve every disturbing bad behavior that disrupts our own security and everybody else's peace of mind. May we listen openheartedly, speak confidently, hug strongly, shake hands with great resolution, honor our children, respect our elders, and take responsibility. It is our structure. We are *one* people, *one* world, and *one* universe.

Expression: Remind yourself of your historical structure handed down through your family and societal patterns. Give yourself permission to confidently be mind-savvy and make new choices. Write a list of these choices.

Appreciate your strength to release
what no longer serves you.

Day 48

Greatness of Heaven

Timeless Wisdom: On the shadow side of the moon, there are more stars than any of us could ever believe. Beyond the greatness of heaven is an infinite gathering of paparazzi with flashing lights. They wait in anticipation for every golden flutter to make the big time. Of course, we all want to walk the red carpet and have a star with our name on the boulevard. Is it possible there could be glory in heaven waiting for a parent, a construction worker, and a teacher? How about a trumpet sounding for a janitor, an auto mechanic, and a nurse? Maybe even a single paparazzo could make it to the top with the right subject matter in her camera's eye. Contact lenses will never do when all the stars in the sky are only reflections in our mirror with blinders on.

Expression: Use your color pencils to draw your own glory days and the dreams you once thought were possible. Make your drawings sparkle.

Express appreciation for the twinkle in your eyes.

Day 49

Get Up and Go

Timeless Wisdom: Chase butterflies across the desert with sand squishing between the toes on a dog day afternoon. We were drinking an energy drink, waiting for nothing in particular, while we sat on a tailgate. There just ain't no reason to give it all up when there is so much we haven't had time to do or see. Our mind sends us looking back at the good ol' days, when the 'here and now' is passing us by. Wait up! Looks like the past has come and gone. Now is the time to go with the gusto and grab our opportunities to be real.

Expression: Write about your present possibilities and what you believe and value. Remind yourself where your heart truly belongs.

Open the door for more moments to demonstrate your gratefulness.

Day 50

Room For Extraordinary

Timeless Wisdom: A new day, another opportunity to envision, recreate our existing circumstance into a healthier, more vibrant world. Within the container of what we believe ourselves to be, where we conceive ourselves to live, work and play, there is room for the extraordinary. Expanding our exceptional visionary skills to embrace greater qualities of self-worth, excellent health, nourishing relationships, superior education, and wholesome environments, we generate a sincerely peaceful world.

Expression: You are on an extraordinary mission in this lifetime. Create a list of words that inspire and express your amazing visions of yourself. Then read your list out loud, and let the vibration of each word nourish you.

Appreciate all your extraordinary talents,
qualities and expressions.

Day 51

Inner Knowing

Timeless Wisdom: In our multi-layered, multi-dimensional day we wander easily, steady as we go, from one project to the next. Often, we don't even notice an infinitesimal adjustment in our multi-tasking, or how simplistic our cellular structure fabricates to propel us on our journey. All of our pieces fit together perfectly, divinely fashioned along destiny's path. When there appears to be a stumble or a struggle, it could be time to move a little slower and look around to see if we have missed a fork in the road. We can depend on our senses, put some trust in our intuition, and listen deeply to our inner guidance before we jump in with both feet. Our path is clearly one of exploration and requires an element of trust in our natural way of being.

Expression: Trust your inner knowing and feel everything in your world fitting together. Write about the sensations you feel in your body when you know you are in sync with your deepest truth.

*Thankfulness creates a trust that you
are on your intuitive path.*

Day 52

Potentials and Possibilities

Timeless Wisdom: Spin the wheel on probabilities, grab a golden ring around a rosy with our pockets full of potentialities, and off we go to the races. Upside down, inside out, and over the rainbow until timeless cat's eye marbles make new rules. Along the mesa's edge we hula-hoop our way over shooting stars and articulate our wishes before the candles on our Texas sheet cake melt into the chocolate buttercream icing. "To bed, to bed," said Sleepy Head. Change is all around us and inevitable. We will take the path of least resistance if we know what is good for us.

Expression: Draw a big circle, and inside the circle draw lines like cutting pieces of a pie. Inside the pie pieces, write some of your potentials and possibilities, and then add more possibilities not in your present existence. Think beyond your definition of reality, and watch for them to show up.

Spin a wheel of thankfulness for pockets full of possibilities.

Day 53

Crossroads

Timeless Wisdom: At the crossroads we notice a path stretched out in front of us. We could keep going, hold everything together, make a few adjustments, be diligent, and do our best to follow through. There is also a road to the left that may be enticing. We could go for broke and leap into the abyss of "what if", put everything behind us, start all over, and do the best we can. We might turn right and look at what is offered there. It may require a massive move with no turning back. No matter which choice we make, past experience tells us we will be at this place again someday. When choices are stressful, standing still may be the best solution. In a day or two, a light will shine brightly on the path and everything will fit into place. We can move forward with confidence.

Expression: Draw a crossroads symbol in the middle of the page. Think about what each direction means to you, and draw a symbol or use a color for each choice. See where a thought or emotional charge may be, and place a check mark next to it. Write a message to yourself and accept your preferred choices without question.

Shout out a "thank you" for all the
'what ifs' you have left behind.

Day 54

Eagles' Grace

Timeless Wisdom: There is a gracefulness floating over us, like a shadow of an eagle as it circles the sky. An eagle's wingspan of seven feet of golden feathers brushing clouds can leave us breathless. We never saw it coming, never knew what left us, a simple heartfelt touch, a kind, generous gift from heaven. A quiet glance back over the eagle's shoulder presented us with an elegant untold story, a subtle ginger-spice harmonic shift, and a miracle in our state of being. It composed a carefree acceptance of what we know about life, a cut above the rest.

Expression: There is a simple grace, being in the right place at the right time, a carefree knowing bestowed with kindness. Write about your miracles, your gifts from heaven, and how you could pay them forward.

*Gracefully express a simple gratitude
for the small gifts of the day.*

Day 55

Personal Point of View

Timeless Wisdom: Where we stand is the axis of time and space, a center post known only from our personal point of view. Our world has become massively clustered in loose change for a soda and a ride on a trolley car. Or maybe if we take a bus full of passengers with ear buds humming unrecognizable tunes it could create some sort of safety net. No one else is watching while we twist the lid off a bottle and fill our veins with predictability. The driver slams on his brakes, and our heads bobble like dancing toys. Wigs, hats and glasses grow cock-eyed, and nary a drop of soda is spilled. For the most part, we all made it through one more day. Jump down, turn around, and put a big grin on our beautiful faces. We stick to the routine and take our places in line.

Expression: Observe your position in and your perspective on the world around you. Shift your point of view, change perspective, add some color, and open the door to a new outlook. Write down feelings that arise for you.

Appreciate your ability to shift your point of view.

Day 56

Awaken Opportunity

Timeless Wisdom: We live in an outrageously pivotal time. We are bombarded with billions of eclectic choices in every breathing moment. Within the turmoil of our inner workings, it all boils down to our grassroots decisions between fear and love. Both love and fear have magical powers surrounded with dust particles. These microscopic love fragments and fear molecules gather together in compatibilities and attract more of the same. Every little daily challenge gives us opportunities to awaken our enlightened courage, shift from fear to love, and stand in what we believe is our truest choice. To paraphrase the great Talmudic scholar Rabbi Hillel the Elder (110 BCE to 10 CE), if I don't act now, when will I ever act?

Expression: Write down your first thoughts upon waking. Were they filled with fear or love? Realize you can choose new thoughts at any moment. Write about a collection of your thoughts.

Empower yourself with gratitude for being mindful.

Day 57

Molding Vision

Timeless Wisdom: The stony, sandy shore receives the ocean with no complaint or resistance, just as we accept morning. May we rise to meet every fresh moment presented to us, look deeper beyond our thoughts, and notice our heartbeat. Let us lead, one foot in front of the other with confidence, faith and trust for every small step we take. The universe greets us with open arms. Everything surrounding us and presented to us is there for a reason. As the potter molds the clay, we have the ability, wisdom and skill to mold our circumstances into our successful vision.

Expression: Imagine your life as a block of clay you can mold any way you wish. What are all the things you would create with the clay? Imagine these items as visions or objects displayed on your shelf for you to admire. Draw, write, or use any materials to depict what you want most.

*Thank the universe for every situation it
offers you with faith and trust.*

Day 58

Rumbling Voice

Timeless Wisdom: A silent rumbling came from inside Mother Earth. It awakened a feeling of unrest in each of us. It stirred a mythic call and gave rise to memory like a dream, a raging river running through each of us. Not one of us could turn away. We each knew the time had come to stand up, speak out, and move forward. The word was out on the street and there was no turning back. We became aware of our authentic destiny even when it appeared unlikely, uncomfortable or unreasonable. We have made the leap of faith, spread our wings, and shouted, "It's our time!"

Expression: It is your time to speak up. What would you love to say? What is the raging river running through you? Give yourself permission to spread your wings. Write a list of words that support your dreams.

Pat yourself on the back and acknowledge your brave heart.

Day 59

First and Last Moment

Timeless Wisdom: We walk in a world where one moment dies and another moment is born. Each moment is effortless from dying to living. Death rides the surface of each wave across a fearless ocean of unknowing. A new beginning happens after something else has ended. Our gardens rise and fall, live and die and live again in a new season without holding onto the past or fighting the flow of nature. We struggle through change, demanding to get our way when there is nothing left to hang onto. Our breathing process is one of giving and receiving, of absolution and a way of letting go for a fresh start. We can empty our footprints along the edge of death's surface, and assimilate our present moment with a new birth. It is ours to live in the now of openheartedness.

Expression: What if our first minute is our last minute all rolled up in one? When do you start living? Choose your favorite colors and doodle about your connection to the best time in your life. A minute may be a lifetime.

Reflect on your lifetime with unending appreciation.

Day 60

Twenty Years From Now

Timeless Wisdom: Living from the core of our innermost soul grants us a confident wisdom to stretch into the future. We grow out of muddy waters, blossom in living color with the tide, and witness destiny unfolding for us and our next generation or two. May we listen for our future's unborn voice as it floats across the sea and jumps from one star to the next. It is time to prepare for the fulfillment of our cosmic destiny.

Expression: Write today's date twenty years into the future. Imagine yourself twenty years older. Write: *"Today, as I sit here writing, I am* (your age twenty years from now)". Now describe where you live and what you are doing. Let your creative muse do the writing.

Express gratitude for being in alignment with your cosmic destiny.

Afterglow

I rose out of embers left behind in ashes of an original fire. There came an authentic rumbling to the questions: who am I and why am I here? The embers smoldered deeply inside the hearts of my ancestors, my relatives, and flowed like lava through every cell in my being. It felt like a natural wandering wind, a voice only I could hear. An utterance rose as an individual lyric, a personal heartfelt duty given to me for safekeeping. I began to write from this deep inner knowing of my natural consciousness.

Very soon after the first inspired oration fell across the keyboard, I recognized this natural voice had always been there, hiding under layers of pain, insecurity, fear, anger and expectations. Ashes coated generations of living, of habits, addictions, customs and obsessions. There were layers of deep wounds rising out of my DNA experiences of genocide, oppression and hardships. The only way through the suffering was to trust in my authentic self, the truth of that being I have always been and yet have never honestly accepted.

Infinite Footprints came out of deep listening to my inner being, a reclaiming and an acknowledging of an ancient truth embedded in my uniquely individual DNA codes. I began learning from that place of truly knowing my soul and I honestly understood my own sufficiency, strength and reason for living.

I began to grasp the importance of a shift in my thoughts and language. In order to know myself *completely*, I had to share these verses with all who were interested in recognizing their own authentic, one-of-a-kind souls.

As I became brave enough to share the passages with friends, many related to them and asked for more. Susan J. Rosenthal approached me with the concept for a book, we joined forces and *Infinite Footprints* rose out of our historical ashes. Our collaboration was based on our shared values, our desire to create a united community of mutual respect to raise consciousness, and in our belief that we had a duty to inspire others to be completely authentic. The opportunity to co-create with Susan gave deliberate meaning to thoughts I had previously penned as we wrote *Timeless Wisdoms, Expressions,* and *Gratitude* mantras within *Infinite Footprints.*

In this collection, you were presented with an opportunity to explore your own sense of self, your truest inner being, and open possibilities that would uplift your consciousness. *Infinite Footprints* was created to renew and replenish your natural gifts with imaginative expressions for you to maintain a confident awakening to the fullness of your greatest instinctual legacy.

When you began to awaken your soulful passions and feel the flames of your inner-wisdom, you may have discovered you had worn a path over a cindered landscape. There may be those of you who meandered around in circles, flipped through pages until you realized it could be time to revisit the original fire. Only you can tend the fires burning in your soul.

Each day offered you wise reflections to ponder, a page for you to explore your own intimate thoughts, and a singular gratitude to carry with you throughout the day. This book was designed for you to better know the fullness of yourself in ways that build your strength, generate your passion, and enhance your evolutionary consciousness.

I personally invite you to rise up out of the live coals that color your life's saga, cultivate and nurture your inner feelings, dreams and voices. Stoke your own fires and rise-up out of your ashes, like the Phoenix of ancient times, out of old family patterns, personal stories, and freely stand in your truest self. Bask in the *afterglow* of self-examination that leads to an awakened life of peace and tranquility.

Tu Bears
Writer, Artist, Oracle

About the Authors

Tu Bears is an award-winning author, poet, artist, ceremonial leader and spiritual guide. She is of Choctaw, Cherokee, and Shakchi Humma Native American heritage. Tu Bears' mission is to encourage, motivate and inspire individuals to live their own sacred life. With her gifts as an oracle and a teacher, she continues to assist many on their journey to self-discovery.

Tu Bears honors her heritage and ancient knowledge with Timeless Wisdoms. The wisdoms were originally written in letters and online, the messages reach thousands of followers, colleagues, authors, teachers, students and professionals around the world who start their day with a note from Tu Bears. Readers share how these musings spark their creative spirit, expand their vision, encourage them to chase new opportunities, and inspire them to transform their being.

Susan J. Rosenthal is an artist, business leader and healer who has held senior positions with Fortune 500 companies, entrepreneurial ventures and non-profit organizations across 100 countries. Susan integrates inspirational and motivational messages in her leadership, speaking, coaching and mentoring with communities worldwide, encouraging others to be their true selves and create a world for the highest good of all.

Susan's spiritual awakening and personal transformation began at nine years old. She received inner guidance to access higher consciousness for herself and others. Susan created and hosted a conference on healing in New York City in honor of the lives lost on 9/11. Featuring numerous speakers and workshops, it offered practices and tools for people to heal and empower themselves, and be the master of their life journey.

Acknowledgements

We wish to acknowledge all of those who contributed, influenced and encouraged us throughout the process of birthing this book.

From the beginning, Lorraine Lima has provided insight, motivation, and creative inspiration. We thank Gary Hawbaker for his support that nourished the soul.

We are sincerely grateful to Laurie McCammon for appreciating our vision and knowing the impact of our universal messages. Laurie's insightful "Enough" message inspires and uplifts us to stand in our individual truth.

We sincerely appreciate the creative artistry of Mikki Fraser and Tamra Dorsey. We also acknowledge our multitude of muses, mentors and role models including Mark Nepo, Julia Cameron, Dr. David Hawkins, Ramana Maharshi, Michael Croft, Jann July, Helen Wells, Dr. Clarissa Pinkola Estes, Linda Sechrist, Frances Wagner, Warner Rosenthal and Bill Burns.

Lastly, we are grateful to our readers, colleagues and clients who choose in each moment to explore their inner selves and express their truest beings by leaving their footprints. They are our community and heroes.

Praise for Infinite Footprints

"*Infinite Footprints*' daily writings are entertaining, inspiring and sacred. They help me live a more intentional, authentic and conscious life, and be my best self everyday."

> – Heather Plett, Author of *A Soulful Year, Pathfinder: A Creative Journal for Finding Your Way, The Spiral Path: A Woman's Journey to Herself and Mandala Journal*, Manitoba, Canada

"Wisdom abounds, and therein lies the joy of the *Infinite Footprints* experience. It is more than just a book; it's a path of self-discovery and self-expression for all."

> – Michael Croft, Fiction Editor, Poet, and Novelist, Nevada USA

"Tu Bears and Susan J. Rosenthal write with an immediacy and simplicity that takes you on a joy-filled ride through your own universe. You feel the writers speaking to you. You see the big, very big picture behind that everyday image of a footprint. They take you into the words and out through the expression of these meanings upon your life and your life's many and varied footprints. If I hesitated to do the exercises, "Expressions", I rebounded with surprise to think through the people to whom

I was most grateful. This book envelops your being. It is far more than just a good read."

> – Dr. David Jenkins, Clinical Psychologist, Author of *Dream RePlay: How to Transform Your Dream Life*, USA/ Thailand

"*Infinite Footprints* helps me set an intention or idea for the day. The timeless wisdoms are often exactly what I need, want to hear, or both. Each expression deepens the experience, and helps me transform myself into the person I am meant to be."

> – Gail West, Marriage and Family Therapist, Adjunct Faculty, Cabrillo College, California USA

"My experience of *Infinite Footprints* is an enlightened feeling of lightness. Each daily message has spiritual meaning grounded in the events of today. The messages give me pause to reflect during the day. At times, they are particularly relevant, and there are other times when they are meaningful as the day progresses. I feel they are soul inspired."

> – Anne Bertucci, Artist, New Jersey USA

"I am influenced by *Infinite Footprints* to peel away the layers of falsehoods that no longer serve me, to dive more deeply into the sparkling, life-giving waters of my truest self, and to soar on silver strands amid the stars. My experience with this book is visceral, resonating throughout my entire being. I find myself feeling relaxed, contemplative, introspective and playful. I heave sighs of gratitude upon each read, absorbed in bliss."

– Paris Almond, Artist and Healer at Art Theraplay, Nevada USA

Infinite Footprints is uplifting, inspirational and truly beautiful! This book creates stunning visualizations."

– Mary Cunningham, International Regional Coordinator and Convener for Gather the Women Global Matrix, Arizona USA

"I love each day's experiential message. I feel myself being led along a path, mindful of my every step. My heart feels lighter with each exercise as my structured illusions are peeled away like layers of an onion. This book is a lovely experience and one I do not want to end."

– David McElhinney, Nevada USA

Infinite Footprints has become an important part of my day. It's how I start my day. I spend a considerable amount of time thinking about the daily message, because so often it's just what I need to hear, consider and ponder. Or it's something I hadn't thought of and am inspired to meditate on the meaning and how it fits into my life, goals, etc."

– Dani Durkee, Nevada USA

"The timeless wisdoms are colorful in their words. They take me to a deeper place inside myself, cause me to slow down and think about things I don't usually think about, and ask me to draw, color, or imagine in ways I don't usually do. I find myself thinking of people I'd like to gift this book to. I don't take time to think about things that these reflections ask me to think about like sitting on a star in the Milky Way and imagining my true self. Meditating on it, drawing, coloring or writing about it takes it to a deeper level."

> – Suzan Nolan, Matrix Convener, Gather the Women Global Matrix, South Dakota USA

"There are many 'pauses' in my day when I focus on each wisdom's meaning and purpose in my life and the lives of those I interact with. *Infinite Footprints* will make a wonderful gift and is recommend to anyone who seeks personal enlightenment."

> – Frances Wagner, Retired English Teacher, Maryland USA

"The possibility, the longing to uncover my true self resonates deeply with me. I feel full of gratitude that *Infinite Footprints* provides a vehicle for that! It is for people who are open, curious to explore the magic that they are, and want pointers, invitations, and impulses to leave the daily routine."

> – AnnaMaria Begemann, Colorado USA

"*Infinite Footprints* offers such a precious heart and soul remembering in these precarious times. It has deep, life-changing potential, and truly reminds us to make our own journey to uncover the sacredness of our lives."

> – Katharina Sebert, Germany

More Praise for
Infinite Footprints

"I highly recommend *Infinite Footprints: Daily Wisdom To Ignite Your Creative Expression in Walking Your True Path* by Tu Bears and Susan J. Rosenthal to all human beings who want to walk their true path with purpose and in a playful, fun way. From the moment I read the preface of the book to participating in the exercises and gratitude statements, I immediately felt an expansion of my own sense of infinite possibilities.

Being a life coach and death midwife, I know how crucial it is to help people navigate the human experience all the way to the end with a sense of ease, grace, dignity and honor (and a lot of humor thrown in). I find *Infinite Footprints* to be a beautiful way of reminding us to stay in touch with our inside life... so our outer life becomes a reflection of our heart and soul's desires and creative expressions.

In doing the exercises so beautifully presented in the book, I was gently reminded of what is important to focus on. By shining a light on how we celebrate ourselves and the people we love, I discovered precious insights about my own journey. Continually reflecting on what I am truly grateful for, how I celebrate myself, who I am now and in the future, and what I am willing to do, reminds me my life is always an inside job.

I feel a renewed sense of excitement and validation in what I already do to celebrate my life. And I have discovered even more wonderful ways to celebrate, expanding upon those possibilities. This book is an extremely valuable tool that reminds us that living a joyful, fulfilled life is here for the taking, and the more time we take to go inside the happier, more joyful and loving our lives become.

Recognizing that whatever we do leaves a footprint behind us, and imagining the ones in front of us, opens up entirely new realities. There's a bit of magic in that dynamic. The gentle messages, along with the poetic articulations of life's possible experiences, were so easy to embrace, embody and implement.

Tu Bears and Susan's energies merge in a most natural way, and what I am left with is a feeling of gratitude. I know my heart and soul were delighted to play on the stage with my imagination, dreaming up fun and delightful things to think about.

Just being reminded to celebrate life is such a huge part of creating the life we truly desire, living from our truest selves. I was most definitely ignited and my creative expression flowed from beginning to end. What they say will happen once you engage in the exercises actually happens. It's as simple as that.

I highly recommend *Infinite Footprints* to those who truly want to walk their path and leave behind their unique footprints through their own creative expression. If that's something you desire this is the book for you!"

– Shelley S. Whizin, Founder, Soul Diving Institute, Author
of *Healing Journal: Celebrating the Fulfillment of the Soul.*

Also Available From

INFINITE
FOOTPRINTS

Courses, life coaching, and the Infinite Footprint Community provide opportunities for readers to further expand on the creative and interactive experience of *Infinite Footprints: Daily Wisdom To Ignite Your Creative Expression in Walking Your True Path.*

Courses: Practical, creative and interactive online and live courses expand the Infinite Footprints messages and tools, deepening the learning and transformational experiences.

Life Coaching: One-on-one and group life coaching programs address individual life purpose, life events, transitions, relationships, career, well-being, finances and other life experiences.

Community: The growing Infinite Footprints Community brings together people from diverse countries and walks of life to expand their knowledge and share experiences through online interactions and live events.

For more information, go to:
Website: www.infinitefootprints.com
Facebook: https://facebook.com/Infinite-Footprints/
Twitter: @infinitefp17
Instagram: https://instagram.com/infinitefootprints/

For speaking, media and press inquiries, please contact:
Info@InfiniteFootprints.com